the haggis

· a little history ·

clarissa dickson wright

· **·** ·

illustrated by clare hewitt

Appletree Press

First published in 1996 by
The Appletree Press Ltd.
19-21 Alfred Street,
Belfast BT2 8DL
Tel. +44 232 243074
Fax +44 232 246756

The Haggis: A Little History

A catalogue record for this book is
available inThe British Library.

ISBN 0-86281-635-1

9 8 7 6 5 4 3 2 1

Clarissa Dickson Wright

"The first *squirt*
of the
haggis
is the hottest"

· contents ·

· introduction ·

In the preparation of this book, many people were surprised to be approached by a large, enthusiastic female asking for five words they associated with Scotland. That was the author of this little book. Three quarters of those asked included the haggis in their selection of words. I then asked one hundred people with what country they associated haggis. With one exception, the answer was Scotland. The exception answered Ancient Greece - but more of that later.

Haggis is not peculiar to Scotland; as we will see, it is a dish that is produced in a variety of forms throughout the world, made with whatever local ingredients come to hand. So why such strong associations with Scotland? After much questioning I was forced back on the obvious answer - Robert Burns. The immortal memory of Scotland's most celebrated poet is maintained at Burns' Night dinners on his birth date of January 25th, and haggis is invariably served, with due recitation of his *Address to the Haggis*. Had he never written it, one wonders what would be on the menu instead? The Haggis and the Immortal Memory have served each other well over the past two hundred years. Incidentally, *Address to the Haggis* (see the Appendix to this book) is by no means a completely innocent ode to a staple food: it has a strongly satirical dimension. But again, more later.

The haggis has been the subject of much ridicule and endless bad jokes. Scotland abounds with picture postcards of humanised haggis, or three-legged haggis being hunted through the heather. But the story of the haggis is worthy of more serious, if not solemn, attention. I hope that among the text that follows you find something to divert, interest and entertain you.

C. D. W.

· what's in the name ·

In his *Complete Dictionary of Etymology*, Professor Skeat treats of the haggis as follows:

> **Haggis**: dish commonly made in a sheep's maw, of minced lungs, hearts, and liver of the same animal.

He assigns a Scandinavian origin to the word, with an Anglo-French suffix. The *hag-* part is Scandinavian, and Skeat links it to Icelandic *hoggva* and *haggw* - to hew. Later, in Norman French, there is a verb *haguer* - to cut up. The modern German *hackwurst* -minced sausage, is from the same stem. Our etymologist also finds various Middle English spellings of the word: *hagas*, *hageys*, *hakkys*. The Gaelic word, *taigeis*, is not native, but borrowed from the same root.

There is a long-standing theory that haggis was a gift of the "Auld Alliance", and that the dish and its name came to Scotland from France at some time in the Middle Ages. The French word *hachis* is seen as the source. Sir Walter Scott is a prime architect of this theory, with King James's cook, in *The Fortunes of Nigel*, assigning the French term *hachis* to the famous Scots delicacy. It is still current in modern times; in the delightful book *Nairn in Darkness and Light*, David Thompson gives this as an example of the French influence on Scottish speech and vocabulary. But it is not true. The doyenne of Scottish food historians,

F. Marian McNeill, felt that the linguistic evidence in favour of Scandinavia was crucial; I share that view, and I shall try to show that the source of haggis is not to be found in France, but in ancient Scandinavia.

Dishes made in the maw of an animal are still found in Scandinavia, and haggis is eaten with relish by Scandinavian visitors to Scotland, who frequently remark on its similarity to some dish in their own local cuisine. The alliance with France certainly goes far back, to William the Lion in the twelfth century, but Scotland's links with the Nordic lands are hundreds of years older than that. By the ninth century, the inhabitants of the islands and the mainland were all too familiar with the Vikings, who at first had been seasonal raiders but soon became permanent settlers. With the settlements came agriculture and trading, and the intermingling of two ways of life. When King Duncan came to the throne of a united Scotland in 1034, a huge tract of the North and all the Hebrides, Orkney and Shetland were not in his realm, but part of the Kingdom of Norway. Gradually the mainland was reclaimed, but it took longer for the Hebrides, and the Northern Isles became part of Scotland only in 1468.

Whether or not the Vikings took haggis with them on their raiding voyages will never be known. But they undoubtedly took their sheep - or other people's - when they settled, and their womenfolk took their traditional

skills and recipes.

Adherents of the French theory may still say this is no proof. After all, the Norsemen established themselves in France as well, hence the name of Normandy. Perhaps the haggis found its way from Norway to Scotland by way of Northern France, when French soldiers and ambassadors began to arrive? But, apart from seeming rather far-fetched, there is the fact that I have yet to find a single dish that resembles haggis in the well-documented culinary history of France. If it was so popular in the Middle Ages, why is it not mentioned, and where has it gone to now? In the years when Paris was the finishing school for the Scots nobility, and training ground for the clergy, the exiles used to have to import it from Scotland. It was known in France as "le pain bénit de l'Ecosse".

· why haggis? ·

It can be difficult, in the age of the microwave oven and the non-stick frying pan, to think of a time when fire was not started at the touch of a button, and was not instantly controllable. Not so long ago, and not least in Scotland, even the most basic cooking utensils were hard to come by. In truly primitive cooking, one of the best things to use as a cooking vessel is the skin of the newly-killed animal. Filled with water and suspended on sticks above the fire, with heated stones added to help the water to boil, it cooks the chopped-up meat. The hot stones need replacing regularly. It works - I have tried it and can vouch for it.

The offal of an animal, as the part that deteriorates fastest, is always eaten first; it is also the most difficult part to carry. One can imagine our ancestor faced with this dilemma. Having slain his beast, he has eaten the liver and kidneys, kebabbed on sticks, and is left with the tripes and lungs. These do not grill well, and are not very appetising when plain-boiled. But he could not afford to waste anything, and there is the stomach of the animal as a ready-made cooking container - after a few explosive experiments, an early form of haggis appears quite naturally.

In a number of countries, Scotland among them, haggis was made with dried or smoked meat. This then becomes

a way of preserving the dish through the winter. The Swedish dish, *Polsa*, is made in this way. Seventeenth-century references allude to the Scottish Highlanders' use of "pleated meat" cooked with oatmeal in an intestinal bag to eke out their supplies of food during the winter months. This seems to refer to a type of biltong or dried meat - undoubtedly from the small, agile black cattle of the old Highland economy: reared on the mountains and driven south to market, for fattening on richer grasses. During times of hardship, the clansfolk supplemented their diet by drawing off blood from their live animals and mixing it with milk and meal, as the Masai, another pastoral people, do to this day.

· what from? ·

Despite the association of haggis with sheep, it is a dish that can be made from other animals. Dorothy Hartley, in her book *Food in England* (1954) refers to **pig haggis:**

> This is very good, especially if you like tripe (in Ireland the tripe was the gift to the labourer who helped kill the pig). The stomach is turned inside out, scrubbed clean, soaked overnight in strongly salted water and then stuffed with potato and sage-and-onion stuffing, sewn up and roasted in the oven, being well basted during the process with bacon fat. It takes 2-3 hours to roast and is served with apple sauce and gravy.

There is also a charming medieval dish of small pig's haggis to be served at a banquet. Some were gilded with a butter of egg and flour; some made green with chopped parsley; some black, using blood; others were spiked all over with split almonds to look like sea urchins, and were thus named "Yrchins".

I have yet to find anyone producing pig's haggis today. The Scots have a possibly Biblical aversion to the consumption of pork; they eat comparatively little of it, and that mainly in the form of ham and bacon. I suspect pig's haggis to have been a largely English or Irish dish.

The Auchtermuchty Deer Farm produces an excellent and very popular **venison haggis**. The umbles or innards of the deer were always the perk of the hunter who made the kill, and though there is no evidence of their having been made into haggis, it is highly likely. Edinburgh's foremost game butcher, George Bower, is of the opinion that all haggis was originally venison-based, and that everything else came later. When I asked him why, he gave me a scathing look and replied "Guid sense!"

John Macsween, of the Edinburgh haggis dynasty, was once judge at a haggis-making competition in Boston, Massachusetts. To his surprise, not one of the entries was a sheep's haggis, and the most amazing was a **chicken haggis**. The chef who had made it had removed the chicken skin, intact, with the breast meat, then stuffed it with minced chicken, giblets and stuffing, and sewed it up and cooked it as a conventional haggis. It won the prize.

Whilst researching the haggis, I came across a recipe for **camel haggis**. This is made with the stomach of the camel, in the traditional way, but with a stuffing of couscous and dried dates. Unfortunately there was no explanatory text attached, so I was unable to discover whether it was an indigenous dish, or the recipe of some homesick Scot, driven to desperation in a desert outpost.

Every year, food enthusiasts and writers gather at the Oxford Food Symposium, and bring unusual dishes to the

Saturday lunch. A few years ago, Julia Child brought some of the staple food of the North American Plains Indians, "pemmican". Any romantic illusions I had about the diet of Geronimo and Sitting Bull were dispelled. Pemmican is dried buffalo tripes and other meat, pounded with fat, and stored in the stomach of the animal. Does this sound at all familiar?

· how old is haggis? ·

Butchers in ancient Rome sold carcases to households *cum intestinis omnibus*, that is to say, with all the insides. This can only have been so that the cook could make good use of them. The comic cook, waving his stuffed bladder, was a familiar figure on the Roman stage as he was, even earlier, on the Greek one. There is a passage in Aristophanes' play, *The Clouds*, in which the cook is busy preparing a feast in which one of the prime features is, undoubtedly, a haggis. There is much slapstick with the sheep's bladder, but in the end, what goes into it, with a few regional variations such as barley and thyme, is the contents of a haggis. The poet's glowing description of it even extols (as Burns did) the golden beads of fat that develop as the haggis cooks. Inevitably, of course, the haggis bursts, as we find in another Greek source, when Strepsiades entertains Socrates with his account of a personal confrontation:

> Why, now, the murder's out!
> So was I served with a stuffed paunch I broiled
> On Jove's day last, just such a scurvy trick;
> Because forsooth, not dreaming of your thunder,
> I never thought to give the rascal vent,
> Bounce goes the bag, and covers me all over
> With its rich contents of such varied sorts...

Despite such intriguing correspondences, I do not think, however, we can prove any direct culinary link between Scotland and Ancient Greece.

· some haggis history ·

The first known English cookery book is *The Form of Cury* (Cookery), written in 1390 by one of the cooks to King Richard II. It contains a recipe for a dish called *Afronchemoyle*, which is in effect a haggis:

> Nym Eyren with al the wyte & myse bred & scheps talwe, get as dyse grynd peper & safron & caste thereto & do hit in the schepys trype. Set it wel & dress it forth.

> Take eggs, with the white and yolk together, and mix with white breadcrumbs and finely diced sheep's fat. Season with pepper and saffron. Stuff a sheep's tripe with the mixture, sewing securely. Steam or boil and drain before serving.

The saffron would give the mixture a golden colour, while the swelling bread would give a firm forcemeat.

The haggis became well-established in the Scottish culinary scene, not as a star dish but as an everyday staple. In *The Social Life of Scotland in the Eighteenth Century*, H. Grey Graham describes the town life of the well-to-do in Glasgow. Men of letters, doctors, merchants "... were allured from their abodes as readily as jovial tradesmen to their favourite taverns, where they could have their much-loved banquets of hen broth, black beans, a haggis, a crab pie, with ample punch..." It was the success of Burns' mock-heroic verses that gave the haggis its special prominence in Scottish life. In 1826, Meg Dods produced *The Cook's and Housewife's Manual*. She was the landlady of the Cleikum Inn, in St Ronan's, near Peebles; which housed the gatherings of the Cleikum Club, one of the many dining clubs which flourished at the time. Sir Walter Scott was among the founders, and its members celebrated the national literature and the national spirit (literal and figurative) and took a gentle, nostalgic, antiquarian interest in old Scots customs. Mistress Dods is a mysterious figure about whom rumours abound. It is quite firmly believed by many in the food world that Scott was the author of her cookery book. Others question her very existence, or suppose her to have been Scott's mistress. These are wild speculations: what is clear is that the Cleikum Club was among the first organisations to organise Burns' Nights. Meg included haggis in her suggested Bill of Fare for St Andrew's Day, Burns' Clubs, or other Scottish National Dinners. Her book gives two haggis recipes. The first is:

"The exact formula by which the Prize Haggis was prepared at the famous Competition of Haggises held in Edinburgh when the Cleikum Haggis carried the stakes and that of Christopher North came in Second:

Sheep's pluck and paunch, beef-suet, onions, oatmeal, pepper, salt, cayenne, lemon or vinegar."

The author's note is interesting:

This is a genuine Scotch Haggis: the lemon and cayenne may be omitted and instead of beef gravy a little of the broth in which the pluck is parboiled may be taken. A finer haggis may be made by parboiling and skinning sheep's tongues and kidneys and substituting these, minced, for most of the lights, and soaked bread or crisped crumbs for the toasted meal. There are moreover sundry modern refinements on the above recipe - such as eggs, milk, pounded biscuits, etc.-but these by good judges are not deemed improvements. Some cooks use the small fat tripes as in making lamb's haggis.

The comments of the runner-up, Christopher North, in his memoirs of another dining club, *Noctes Ambrosianae*, shed light on this event:

A dozen of us entered our haggises for a sweepstakes and the match was decided at worthy Mrs Ferguson's, High Street. My haggis (they were all made either by our wives or our cooks at our respective places of abode) ran second to Meg Dods'. The Director General's (which was what sporting men would have called a roarer) came in third - none of the others was placed.

"Christopher North" was the nom de plume of John Wilson, Professor of Moral Philosophy at Edinburgh University. Clearly the haggis was taken seriously in Georgian Edinburgh, though it may be noted that the gentlemen did not in fact take any part in preparing "their" haggis at all. Meg Dods' second recipe is for "Haggis Royal", taken from the Minutes of the Cleikum Club:

Mutton, suet, beef marrow, bread crumbs or oatmeal, anchovies, parsley, lemon, pepper, cayenne, eggs, redwine.

Three pounds of leg of mutton chopped, a pound of suet chopped, a little or rather as much beef marrow as you can spare, the crumb of a penny loaf (our own nutty browned oatmeal, by the way, far better), the beat yolks of four eggs, a half pint of red wine, three mellow fresh anchovies boned, minced parsley, lemon grate, white pepper, crystals of cayenne to taste - crystals alone ensure a perfect diffusion of the flavour - blend the ingredients well, truss them neatly in a veal caul, bake in a deep dish, in a quick oven, and turn out. Serve hot as fire, with a brown gravy and venison sauce.

We have come quite some way from simple cottage fare. This is prosperous Edinburgh's version of Marie Antoinette's "Let them eat cake".

Not all haggis in Scots recipe books is made with a sheep's paunch. There is Haggis in a Jar - "the haggis may be put in a buttered jar or basin instead of the bag, and steamed for four hours. It should not be too moist." Closely related is Haggis in the Pan - "haggis may be cooked like a stew in a saucepan. It has to be stirred occasionally and kept sufficiently moist to prevent it sticking to the bottom of the pan". Somehow, it seems lacking in romance.

To bring the haggis up to date, here is a modern recipe from Dorothy Hartley:

A sheep's paunch and pluck, some of the porous lung, liver and heart, and sometimes the kidneys. Take the suet from around the kidneys and chop it finely. Add about a pint of medium oatmeal, a good amount of chopped onion, a tablespoon of salt, a strong dash of black pepper, half a nutmeg, a handful of currants, raisins or any available fruit element (small wild damsons or garden currants). Mix and pack into the paunch. The secret of making a good haggis is to allow for the swelling-up meal to fill the elastic stomach tightly without bursting. It may be necessary to prick the haggis slightly when

the boiling is beginning, to let out the air. It is easier to sew it up, though the correct fashion is to wrap the stomach over, using wooden skewers."

· the haggis at war ·

In 1746, after the Battle of Culloden, a small group of Jacobite soldiers led by James Moir, Laird of Stoneywood, were on the run. They had paused on the slope of Bennachie to light a fire and cook themselves a meal, thinking themselves safe from pursuit. Just as they were cooking a haggis in a pot, they were surprised by a troop of Hanoverian soldiers.

As they sprang up to flee, the pot was overturned and the haggis rolled out. An English trooper caught it on his bayonet, whereupon the haggis disintegrated, showering him and his companions with its boiling hot contents, temporarily halting the chase.

As the refugees made their escape, one of Stoneywood's companions, John Gunn, called out in Gaelic:

"Even the Haggis, God bless her, can charge downhill!"

· puddinG or sausaGe? ·

What's the difference? Sometimes it can be hard to say. Sausages and meat puddings are both made from meat and normally produced in some sort of casing. But not all sausages are cased, and some puddings are simply boiled in a cloth. However, whilst sausages are sold uncooked, puddings are part-boiled before they are sold. There is a well-established Scottish family of offal puddings, beginning with haggis and continuing through black pudding, white pudding and hog's pudding, which are always cased, and most usually bulked out with some form of grain. The main French offal dish, *andouillette*, is definitely a sausage, in that once its contents are cleaned and cased, it undergoes no further cooking before sale. Burns hails the haggis as a chieftain among puddings, and though it remains supreme, the Scots remain keen eaters of various sorts of meat puddings.

· who makes it? ·

Anyone can make it, with determination and the
necessary ingredients. It may be easier if you live on
a sheep farm and have a large, farm kitchen. But most
people buy their haggis ready-made, even ready-cooked.

Until recently, most butchers did their own slaughtering,
and except in large towns, this was done right behind the
butcher's shop. Consequently, in Scotland and the North
of England, most butchers made their own haggis. This
tradition has remained very much alive in Scotland, and it
is only in recent years, partly due to the complicated
regulations concerning the use of offal, that some
butchers are buying in stock from wholesale producers. I
for one will be sad if the individuality of haggis-making
dies out. One of my favourite haggis suppliers is in fact an
Englishman, married to a Scot, who is a butcher in
Edinburgh. His shop is in Morningside, home of Muriel
Spark's fictional Miss Jean Brodie, and a byword for
refinement and respectability, so I was somewhat taken
aback to be confronted, on my first visit, with a steaming
tray of newly-made haggis. He makes them once a week
and has no trouble at all in disposing of them.

Not far away is the palace of haggis: the premises
of Macsween of Edinburgh, a legendary name in the
international distribution process whereby the haggis
follows the exiled Scot around the world. John Macsween

is a Scottish patriarch: on my visit at 7.30 in the morning he looked as though he had already been at his desk, trading haggis, for hours. His father came to Edinburgh as a young man and found employment as a butcher in a superior establishment in George Street. There he learned haggis-making and in due course became an independent butcher in Bruntsfield, and taught his skills to his son, who added considerable business acumen of his own. A canny man, John Macsween realised that a High Street butcher's business would suffer with the advent of supermarkets, and looked around for a specialisation. Haggis was one of his best-selling lines, so he set out to carve a haggis-shaped niche in the international food business. Today, if you buy a haggis not made by an independent butcher, it is most likely to be one of Macsween's.

Harrods, Fortnum & Mason, and many other grand emporia, stock his wares.

The largest haggis they have yet produced was made by Macsweens for the Scottish Tourist Board in 1970 - a 52-pounder. John Macsween believes that the reason for his firm's success lies in the consistent quality of his ingredients, as well as in the special blend that defines his own product. Like the whisky distiller, he has to satisfy a a fickle public which expects uniformity from a foodstuff which can subtly vary with each different making.

Despite his stature as the world's leading haggis maker, Macsween ran the risk of offending Scotland's haggis purists - of whom there are many - when he responded to a challenge from Tessa Ransford, founder of the Scottish Poetry Library, to produce a vegetarian haggis. This was not an easy thing to do; not much easier than making a non-alcoholic whisky; but Macsween rose to the challenge, and the vegetarian version has thrived. As a traditionalist myself, I prefer the original version, but more than fifteen per cent of Macsween's sales are now accounted for by the vegetarian haggis.

Macsween have moved into shiny new state-of-the-art premises in South Edinburgh, but my introduction to the kingdom of the haggis was in their former home in Bruntsfield. The first room I saw had two vast stainless steel vats in which simmered huge quantities of lambs' lungs. These had been cooking since one o' clock in the

morning. Thermometers on the vats registered that the correct temperature had been attained. James Macsween, of the third generation in the business, showed me an uncooked lung and a cooked one, to display how the texture was altered in the prolonged simmering. Another vat held the beef body fat that was to be mixed with the lungs. Cranes carried the meats, cooked and drained, to mincing machines where they would be mixed in due proportion with the dried onions, the oatmeal (both of the pin and the fine variety), the salt and pepper, the nutmeg, the coriander, all stored ready for use in great sacks and jars.

The lambs are Scottish, processed in Ireland. The dried onions are from Turkey, because no-one in Scotland produces them (for Heaven's sake: the Romans imported onions from Kelso!). The casings come from Germany because British government restrictions have killed off the local trade. I mused on the thought that Macsween alone use £8,000 worth of casings a month, to say nothing of all the other haggis producers in Scotland.

Floundering to regain my sense of romance, I saw a photograph on the wall, of a man busily engaged in stuffing a haggis. James Macsween told me that this man was the former head haggis maker, a stern figure who used to chase the youthful James out of the fascinating haggis rooms whenever he sidled in. The forbidden rooms acquired a magic quality for the little boy, and despite graduating from University in Physical Education, he ultimately returned to the haggis kitchen and became a full-time haggis-maker. He spoke with feeling of the variations in textures and taste, of the many experiments they had carried out with the help of such outstanding food experts as Derek Cooper, until they felt that the ideal balance had finally been achieved.

He made me feel the mixture, both spiced and unspiced; and the texture. A sense of romance was fully restored, as I listened to James enthuse about his subject, feeling that in this young man's dreams the haggis remains something more than a mere product. Haggis production is labour intensive: the mixture is piped in measured quantities into the hand-held casing, and each haggis is cut and clipped by hand. Two men work side by side at this task, chatting about football, films and other mundane things as they create a dish as old as humanity. The haggis are carefully cooked to swell out the skins, and then taken straight to the shop, or are boxed for freezing, or for sending to the far corners of the earth. I heard how today only the "luxury" haggis is still supplied, hand-sewn, in a sheep's stomach. Thus the cottar's simple fare becomes the

epicure's delicacy.

There is no doubting the genuine fondness for haggis among the Scots. Of course, to the distraction of Macsween and other haggis producers, there are the two great annual peaks of St Andrew's Night and Burns' Night, when supply struggles to keep up with demand. During the Gulf War, a tonne of haggis was shipped out to the Scottish troops in their desert encampments. But haggis is also an everyday dish, and displays its versatility in different ways. Fish and chip shops, and even Chinese takeaways, offer a haggis deep-fried in batter, which I find indigestible but which they assure me is a popular item. Haggis certainly crosses the gastronomic barriers. The leading pasta specialist in Edinburgh, Gourmet Pasta, makes a haggis ravioli. Originally commissioned by the luxurious Caledonian Hotel, it is now supplied to other restaurants and to the general public. James Thompson, owner of one of Edinburgh's most stylish restaurants, The Witchery by the Castle, says: "Haggis has got an image problem; many quality restaurants are frightened to serve it lest they should be tarred with the 'tat, tartan, and tourism' brush. We serve a haggis starter with neeps and potatoes because we feel that people like the opportunity to taste it. It remains constantly on the menu which it would not do if it were not a good seller."

· the trimmings ·

Haggis is traditionally served up with mashed turnip and mashed potatoes, "neeps and tatties", though as we have seen, it is vastly older than either vegetable. The turnip in Scotland is commonly brassica rapa, rutabaga or Swedish turnip, in England called the swede. It was introduced to Scotland in the late eighteenth century by Patrick Miller of Dalswinton. He was a wealthy man, a director of the Bank of Scotland and Chairman of the Carron Iron Company, and had a passionate interest in mechanical and agricultural improvement.

King Gustav III of Sweden was a satisfied customer of Carron, and he presented Miller with a gold, diamond-encrusted snuff-box bearing a miniature of himself, containing rutabaga seeds. In this way the "swede" came to Scotland. The box and its accompanying letter can still be seen in the British Museum. By coincidence, Miller was also a friend and patron of Robert Burns, who at one time rented a farm from him, so he and the Bard may have been among the very first consumers of haggis and neeps.

The potato had come to Scotland nearly two hundred years earlier, but had taken a long time to become accepted. Austere Presbyterians pointed out that it was not mentioned in the Bible and it was seen as a luxury food for the rich. It only gradually became established as a staple food during the eighteenth century, replacing or

supplementing the traditional oatmeal. Eventually, of course, it became a prime item in the diet, making the potato famines of the nineteenth century almost as disastrous in Scotland as they were in Ireland.

The Scots are still connoisseurs of the potato, interested in the different varieties, and scorning the simple division into "reds" and "whites", but just when the great triumvirate of haggis, neeps and tatties came together is not recorded. It had certainly become the norm by Victorian times.

A propos of this, I sometimes wonder if nutritionists ever think laterally about what they write. On the one hand they advise us to eat oats for our cholesterol, oily fish for our metabolism, strong green vegetables for their iron, and offal for vitamin A. On the other hand, they condemn the old Scots diet of oatmeal, herring, kale, and haggis (a source of vitamin A), and the potatoes and turnips, providing vitamin C and carbohydrates!

· haggis throughout the world ·

Sweden

It seems only fair to begin in Scandinavia, where the dish received its name. The renowned Swedish food writer Lee Persson told me that every year she brings a group of Swedes, usually university professors and their like, to Scotland. At some point in the course of their tour they encounter haggis. "Ah, Polsa!" they cry, and fall on it with alacrity. Polsa is an early Swedish dish from the countryside. It is made in beef intestine casing, from smoked beef pluck and tripes. The meal used is barley, and there is the interesting addition of lingan berries (compare Dorothy Hartley's recipe using damsons or other fruit). Swedish Polsa is usually made in a pan these days, and is colloquially known as "Freudian slips"; but the history remains. Elsewhere in Scandinavia the name polsa has become corrupted; the Danes use it to refer to their large, red, saveloy-type hot-dogs.

Russia

The Scots association with Russia is long-established; there are records of trading at least as far back as the thirteenth century. Indeed the wandering Scots pedlar with his pack and tray was for centuries a familiar figure across much of Northern Europe. In Moscow, the dialect word for a trader is "Scot". On a grander note, Scottish architects and engineers created both palaces and factories for Imperial Russia. There does not appear to be a native Russian version of haggis, but these pioneers left behind a taste for haggis which still makes Russia one of the biggest importers. Of course, the haggis-Burns connection helps. Russian democrats have always admired the poet of "A Man's a Man for a' That", and the cult of the Burns' Supper flourishes there.

Sir Charles Fraser, former Pursebearer to the Queen, tells of a memorable visit to Russia during the Communist era, when fifty Scots, including Sir Fitzroy Maclean, joined Russian Burns enthusiasts at a Burns' Supper in the Kremlin. There were pipers, singers and fiddle-players in the Scots party. Toasts were drunk in whisky and in vodka, and the haggis was duly addressed and consumed. The Scots were astonished at the evident familiarity of their hosts with the works of Burns. After dinner, the Scots pipers were joined by pipers from Georgia, where the bagpipe is also played by mouth chanter, and a ceilidh developed that lasted long into the night.

Japan

The links between Scotland and Japan are less easy to trace than in the previous examples. Whatever the cause, the effect is there, including pedestrian crossing lights that play Scots tunes while holding back the walkers. And another story of Sir Charles Fraser's concerns a Japanese industrialist at the opening ceremony of a new, Japanese-owned factory in Scotland. After thanking the assembled dignitaries, he threw down the rest of his prepared speech and broke into a full-voiced rendition of "Coming through the Rye", ending to thunderous applause. Macsweens have a Japanese customer who has virtually no English, but has mastered the *Address to the Haggis* in broad Scots and enjoys reciting it, in full Highland dress.

America

There are of course a great many Americans of Scottish extraction, and many of them maintain links with the land of their ancestors. Godfrey Macdonald, Chief of Clan Donald, and his wife Claire, the brilliant cook and cookery writer, go every year to the USA. Lord Macdonald takes his extended chiefship very seriously,

setting forth from Kinloch Lodge Hotel, which is also their family home, and visiting clan societies throughout the world. He, too, found himself having to address a vegetarian haggis; as a confirmed lover of the real thing, he was somewhat nonplussed, but Scots diplomacy prevailed, though he confided to me that it was one of the most horrible things he had ever been forced to eat.

American laws on food importing are very strict. Genuine Scots haggis cannot be bought in the United States. One exile used to have it sent out to her labelled as "modelling clay", and there are tales of the diplomatic bag, that legendary, and much-abused container, bringing supplies to the British Embassy.

Bahrain

Haggis in the Gulf! A group of Scottish expatriates had organised a Burns' Night dinner for their Arab guests. The haggis was delivered in good time, and all else was ready, when the piper, a member of a regiment stationed in Bahrain, was summarily required elsewhere. Distraught at the thought of their haggis being borne in unaccompanied by the wail of the pipes, the organisers hastily made some phone calls, and rigged up a telephone link with a barracks in Scotland. At the appointed hour, thousands of miles away, a piper marched up and down, blowing lustily, and was duly reproduced on loudspeakers in the

dining room.

A haggis turned up in the Saudi Arabian postal system just as the Iraq/Kuwait war was flaring up. It was impounded, under suspicion of being a bomb. The addressees explained what it was, and what it was used for, but the authorities were profoundly unconvinced. Eventually it began to go bad, but the postal authorities, now belatedly convinced that it was, or had been edible, returned it to the senders in Invergordon.

Central Africa

Ian Willox, the radio and television director, grew up in a Scots home in what is now Zambia. His mother experimented long and hard to produce a haggis, but due to a temperamental Aga, the results most often had to be scraped off the kitchen wall. At last a solution was found. Annual leaves were timed so that the return coincided with St Andrew's Night. The returning traveller was responsible for the safe delivery of the haggis. One District Commissioner carried his all the way on his knee, lest it should come to harm.

The Returning Tourist

Many of the hundreds of thousands of tourists who come to Scotland each year, go away with a haggis.

Scottish tradesfolk have learned how to supply this market and minimise the risk of the contents of a suitcase being permeated with the fragrant ingredients we have already been introduced to. In Invergordon, the Highland port where many cruise ships call, there is a remarkable shop called the Cook's Cupboard. It sells such delights as Orkney Black Pudding, made with sheep's blood; bilberry jam from locally-picked berries; and something the proprietor, Norma van Weegen (pure Scots despite the name) refers to as "The Baggis". This is simply a haggis, vacuum-packed in a tartan bag, and it is immensely popular, especially with the Scandinavian customers.

some notable haggis enthusiasts ·

Queen Victoria, an enthusiast for most things Scottish, consumed haggis at least once, and commented: "I find I like it very well." Her descendant, the present Princess Royal, visiting the Royal Highland Show, brought nothing away but a haggis; it was noted that she did not hand it to her Lady in Waiting: a sure sign that she intended to keep it for herself.

Mel Gibson, Australian film-star, having played fast and loose with some of the prime ingredients of Scottish history in his film *Braveheart*, wanted to know how to make haggis, and was filmed achieving this feat during an early morning television programme.

Gavin Hastings, Scotland's own Captain Marvel, was said to lead the Scottish rugby team to victory on haggis.

Thespians, musicians, and politicians have admitted to their appreciation of haggis. What else could unite such a varied collection of people as Rab C. Nesbitt, Malcolm Rifkind, Gloria Hunniford, Windsor Davies, Hank Wangford, Terry Scott and Terence Stamp (though in his case the vegetarian sort only)? But, of course, one admirer of haggis stands far above all the others.

· ROBERT BURNS AND THE HAGGIS ·

It was on his first visit to Edinburgh, in 1786, that Burns wrote his *Address to the Haggis*, its cheerful, vigorous, broad Scots in marked contrast to some of the rather stilted verses he wrote at that time to please the literary establishment of the capital. No doubt he and his fellow-countrymen, at all levels of society, ate a good deal of haggis, but it is most unlikely that he could have realised what the effect of this poem, by no means one of his finest, was to be.

Scotland and England had joined to become the United Kingdom eighty years before, and many of the more genteel members of Scottish society were taking lessons in correct English pronunciation and anxiously trying to lose the distinguishing marks of centuries of Scottish culture and tradition. Burns, a master satirist and profoundly patriotic Scot who detested pretension, was keenly and critically aware of this tendency, and takes it to pieces in the poem. *Address to the Haggis* is democratic, patriotic, atmospheric, and entirely suitable for declaiming in a loud voice. No wonder it has survived triumphantly.

Burns' Night is a focal point of the Scottish year, not just in Scotland but wherever those of Caledonian descent are found. What all these Burns' Clubs and Societies do in the rest of the year I have not been able to discover. Answers have varied from "Oh, it's just an excuse for a

bevvy," to the more mysterious "It's like the Freemasons, ye ken". But the Burns' Night itself has its established ritual, which the poet himself would perhaps have both liked and laughed at. The undoubted centrepiece is the haggis, borne in on a silver platter by the chef, preceded by a kilted bagpiper. Lesser mortals follow, bearing in the dishes of swede and potato. The *Address* is duly recited, and the haggis is then ceremoniously stabbed with the *sgean dhu*, or black knife, kept in the Highlander's stocking. Traditionally, large amounts of whisky are consumed at the same time; indeed an earlier version of the last verse of the *Address* refers to "great John Barleycorn's heart's bluid" being drunk as an accompaniment to the haggis, so this is by no means an unauthorised marriage of two of Scotland's most celebrated products.

· appendix ·

Address to the Haggis

Fair fa' your honest, sonsie face,
Great Chieftain o' the Puddin'-race!
Aboon them a' ye tak your place,
                    Painch, tripe or thairm:
Weel are ye wordy o' a grace
                    As lang's my arm.

The groaning trencher there ye fill,
Your hurdies like a distant hill,
Your pin wad help to mend a mill
                    In time o' need,
While thro' your pores the dews distil
                    Like amber bead.

His knife see Rustic-labour dight,
An' cut you up wi' ready slight,
Trenching your gushing entrails bright
      Like onie ditch;
And then, O what a glorious sight,
      Warm-reekin', rich!

Then, horn for horn they stretch an' strive,
De'il tak the hindmost, on they drive,
Till a' their weel-swalled kytes belyve
      Are bent to drums;
Then auld Guidman, maist like to rive,
      Bethankit hums.

Is there that owre his French ragout,
Or olio that wad staw a sow,
Or fricassee wad mak her spew
      Wi' perfect sconner,
Looks down wi' sneering, scornfu' view
      On sic a dinner?

Poor devil! See him owre his trash,
As feckless as a withered rash,
His spindle-shank a guid whip-lash,
                         His nieve a nit;
Thro' bluidy flood or field to dash,
                         O how unfit!

But mark the Rustic, haggis-fed,
The trembling earth resounds his tread,
Clap in his walie nieve a blade:
                         He'll mak it whissle;
An' legs, an' arms, an' heads will sned,
                         Like taps o' thrissle.

Ye Pow'rs, wha mak mankind your care,
And dish them out their bill o' fare,
Auld Scotland wants nae skinking ware
                That jaups in luggies;
But, if you wish her gratefu' pray'r,
                    Gie her a Haggis!

Robert Burns, 1759 - 1796

· GLOSSARY ·

sonsie: bright, cheerful
painch: paunch
thairm: intestine
wordy: worthy
trencher: wooden serving dish
hurdies: limbs
pin: securing pin
onie: any
horn: horn spoon
weel-swalled kytes: well-filled bellies
belyve: by and by
rive: tear, split
Bethankit: Lord be thanked
staw: overfill
sconner: disgust
rash: reed
nieve: fist
nit: nut
walie: brawny
sned: shear off
taps o' thrissle: thistle-heads
skinking: watery, thin
jaups: slops
luggies: wooden bowls with handles